I Lived Minutes Of Death

Based on true incident

Sumaiyya Jagirdar

ISBN 978-93-5559-163-0
© Sumaiyya Jagirdar 2022
Published in India 2022 by Pencil

A brand of
One Point Six Technologies Pvt. Ltd.
123, Building J2, Shram Seva Premises,
Wadala Truck Terminal, Wadala (E)
Mumbai 400037, Maharashtra, INDIA
E connect@thepencilapp.com
W www.thepencilapp.com

DISCLAIMER: *The opinions expressed in this book are those of the authors and do not purport to reflect the views of the Publisher.*

Author biography

Sumaiyya was born on 9th March. An engineer by profession and loves to do creative things like writing, painting, sketching, crafting, henna designing, etc. She is the founder of Henna Design World and SN Graphics.

CONTENTS

Foreword

Tara, a working woman attempting to balance her work and personal lives, is involved in an accident on a rainy night in Bangalore while driving home from the office in heavy traffic.

She was hit by a car in a traffic light and died minutes later; people around her stood looking at her laying on the road with a bike on her leg, but no one came forward to help her.

She wrote a book about her worst day experience and accident to erase the bad memory of that day from her mind because it was bothering her all the time, that accident and the deadliest experience witnessed that day laying the road.

Tara wanted to destroy what she had written in a book, but the author of the book asked her to write a story about the accident instead.

Tara's story is very interesting, and it is the most interesting. The most intriguing aspect is how the author met Tara and what inspired her to write this book.

Preface

When I read Tara's book, I felt that this story should not be destroyed, but rather shared with readers. Tara wrote a book to destroy the story in her mind, but when I read it, my mind told me that this story is not meant to be destroyed.

This story relates to many working women and has a good awareness message about how one should behave when witnessing an accident and what goes through one's mind when one is on the verge of death.

Acknowledgements

I'd like to express my heartfelt gratitude to my parents, Dr. B. M. Jagirdar and Shamshad Jagirdar, as well as my husband, Mr. Nawaaz, for encouraging me to write this wonderful book (I Lived Minutes Of Death), which also helped me improve my writing and taught me so much.

Second, I'd like to thank my siblings for their assistance in completing this book in such a short period.

CATCHING BUS

One fine morning I needed to go to the workplace by city transport because my bike's rear-wheel was penetrated, the bus station was 1.5 km away from my home.

Climate was frigid cold, even though I wore a coat scarf still I could feel the coldish wind, which made me shudder, the street was generally unfilled, shops were as yet shut, normally, shops get open later 9 am in the Bangalore yet a couple of shops like milk dairy, pastry kitchen gets open early yet that day I saw just milk dairy was open, I thought to get a few treats from the bread shop however the pastry kitchen wasn't yet open.

I was walking on the footpath, an old woman came to me selling blossoms, saying take a few blossoms in the Kannada language ("hoovu tagolamma") I would have rather not buy blossoms so I told her that I am wearing a scarf, I don't wear blossoms so I don't need, however, she demanded me to buy, I denied, then, at that point, she began persuading me saying view these blossoms, at any rate, paying attention to this I checked out her bushel and it was loaded up with exceptionally delightful and new blossoms Jasmine, red roses, pink roses, water drops on those blossoms were looking so wonderful, taking a gander at those blossoms I got a grin on the face she saw my smile and she told without yourself, buy for others

I told her (Ajji implies grandmother in Kannada) that I don't want to give it to others also. Paying attention to me she answered alright ma leave in a soft tone, I felt terrible taking a look at her pitiful face, I chose to get a few and requested that she give me a few blossoms.

I took flowers recalling regarding that woman that while we youngsters are feeling a lot of cold even in the wake of covering ourselves from top to toe however that old woman isn't wearing any comfortable garments, she is simply wearing a cotton saree and selling flowers in such energy of carrying on with life and buckling down.

She gave them with no cover, gave her money, and requested that she give cover, plastic is restricted so don't have covers said old lady, I asked her how would I carry them now to the workplace? put them in a bag, that woman said and left from that point looking for another customer.

I was unable to place taken care of because she has sprinkled water on blossoms and I had an office PC taken care of so I was unable to face the challenge, I looked through my sack, fortunately, I observed one be little cover in my bag, I put those blossoms in cover and the cover clinched and strolled towards the bus station.

After reaching the bus stop I saw people crowded there, unaware why people gathered at the bus stop. I have traveled many times by bus before but never saw such a crowd at this bus stop.

Wondering what might have happened there, I went to a lady standing at the bus stop and asked her, hello aunty, why is there so much crowd today? She gave an angry look, her wide-open eyes looking at me like she will give me a tight slap, I was not expecting that reaction, I got scared and took a step back, she replied sarcastically, why do you want to know? Why do people come to the bus stop? You have come here to catch a bus right? like that even they have come saying this lady looked at her wristwatch, checking the time, holding her hand near her face, she was wearing specs, struggling to see time from that small wristwatch she wore.

Well not sure whether she got to know the time or not but by her rude reply I just bent my neck down and went to the other side of the bus stop with back steps. I think her day started on a bad note, or she might have gotten angry with me for addressing her as aunty.

Well, she looked like she was in her 50s that is why I addressed her as aunty, huge red bindi on her forehead seemed like a red light to me. I don't know exactly what was wrong with her but my morning got a bit bitter by her rude. answer and I decided that in the future I will never ask anything strangers, especially ladies.

Pitiful to observe the way that how might a person be so discourteous to a stranger. Regardless of whether she had an awful morning or even managed more regrettable things however being quiet is better compared to being discourteous.

Meanwhile, a girl wearing a uniform, standing next to that woman came hurrying to me and said Akka (Sister) today 4 bus have not come which should come on time so all are waiting for the bus. Thank you so much kiddo I replied to that cute little girl.

Hearing that girl, I learned the situation, and it appears that even that lady is angry for the same reasons. The fact that some people get upset when they can't make it on time is obvious, but being rude to someone you don't know is still not okay. Whatever, it was my fault that I asked the wrong lady the wrong question at the wrong time. I apologize for my behavior.

The cold had left my hands numb. I rubbed both hands together and felt a little warmth in them. I took my phone out of my bag. It was 7 am.

At this time, I should have been on a bus to reach my office on time, as I would still need to catch one more bus after reaching the Majestic bus stop in Kempegouda. Majestic is the main city bus stop from where we can take buses to all areas in the city.

Since the bus had not yet arrived, I decided to check my phone until it did. Unfortunately, I accidentally opened the camera of my phone and saw my face, making me feel disgusted. My face looks terrible when the front camera opens by accident. I took the picture from a good angle now I look better, though I notice my nose has turned light red from the cold.

Suddenly people started screaming and running I looked around in amazement. What happened? It was a us coming from afar and all the people standing around ran up and gathered at the place where the bus stopped.

I quickly put my phone in my pocket and ran to the bus boarding point when the bus arrived people started jostling each other to catch the bus during the fight to get on us someone hit me in the face with lunch box, it got hurt badly so I took step back holding my right cheek.

Everyone was still fighting to get on us and the driver was asking everyone to calm down saying two more buses coming right behind this one. But people didn't even hear, I just sat on a bench and rubbed my cheek, and the bus drove off with as many people as any truck that transports animals.

That girl came to sit next to me, the one who told me about the crowd, I asked her what is your name? She replied my name was Rakshita and what is your name? I replied by rubbing my cheek my name is Suma. She was eating chocolate so I asked her why are you eating chocolate so early in the morning? unwrapping the remaining chocolate from the left hand, I missed my breakfast today so I am eating chocolate said rakshita. I asked can I know why didn't you have your food? Well my mother prepared upma today and I don't like it yet all that's why I skipped breakfast today, sadly said rakshita.

Fine but why didn't you go on that bus? she replied, haven't you seen so many people get on that bus? At peak times like this, "I don't even try to get on the bus, I'm so small, those ladies will kick me out" she said, Good that you didn't try to get on that bus, look at me, I attempted like a numb-skull and got hit by somebody, check out my cheek. "haha Akka your cheek became red" she laughed. yeah, my nose is already red because of cold and now my cheek got red because of some women, am I looking like a joker? "haha yes yes" she belly laughed.

I was a little irritated by the rudeness of that angry lady and hit by another woman but that girl made my state of mind light, her smiling face erased negative vibes there, her earthy colored eyes had a radiance, she was wearing a white shirt and a navy blue bind with light blue stripes on it, a navy blue colored knee-length skirt, black shoes. I remembered my school days, had a decent discussion with her.

I asked her, why didn't you have your breakfast today? "mother prepared upma today and I hate eating upma", she whispered sadly. I felt bad about that and I suggested to her - "Next time whenever your mother prepares upma, you ask her to prepare something else for you". She drew in a long breath and spoke "You don't know about my mother, she is exceptionally strict, whatever she tells is final in our home".

It's not that I don't think moms are strict, they are mindful, guess what? Mummys consistently make the best decision for kids and upma isn't that awful. It would be great if you listen to your mom, even if you don't like something just talk to her, she will understand you. "Fine I will" she murmured.

The bus was not coming and talking to her made me feel good, continuing our conversation I asked her, Which class do you study in? She tossed a pony over her shoulder and said " I am in sixth class". do you know kiddo? " you are ver cute" I praised her. "Am I cute?" she wondered "

However, my mother consistently lets me know I am mischievous"

She was shaking her legs while talking and changing her hands adjusting her backpack. She asked, "What did your mother cook for you today?", I replied "I am married so I stay with my better half so I need to prepare my food"

with curiosity, she said "Wow then you may prepare whichever food you need to eat right? Indeed, even I need to get married" laughing at her innocence "Haha you are extremely entertaining as well, however, you are so young for marriage". With a low voice she murmured "leave it and what did you eat today for breakfast?", I replied I have prepared but couldn't have it, I will have it in the office in my break time".

She offered me chocolate saying "I eat chocolates when I miss the food, you also eat chocolate Akka, take this, I have one more in my pack, I will eat that", I fell in love with her, she was so adorable, I thanked her "No I can not eat chocolate but thank you kiddo", wonderingly I asked her " you are so relaxed, are you not getting late for school? I am getting tense because am getting late for the office". with a cool gesture, she replied, "I am getting behind schedule for school however it isn't my fault, it is the transport's issue".

Listening to her I felt we elders take everything seriously, few things can be taken easy and make it less stressful, though she was getting late she kept herself calm, but I was taking so much tension, Wanted to know how she would react to missing her school so I asked her "What if you miss your school time?". She hung her head mumbled "

My school begins at 8 am, take a gander at the time on my watch it's 08:05 am, it implies I previously got late, so I can't go to class now, so I will return home", she replied.

I asked her "For what reason are you staying here" rakshita replied "I will spend some more time sitting here and then go back home" wondering why she would do that I questioned her " but why are you not going home?" She drew in a long breath and spoke "I told you na Akka my mom is strict, she will first scold me as I go home, she will not understand that it's the bus fault, she will blame me. I have to get scolded anyway so I will spend some more time here and go back."

She had so much running in her head yet was able to handle the situation lightly, I said to her "You are so young but have so much running in mind, go home, and be nice with your mom, listen to her, now go." She wasn't ready to go and she told with a low voice " I am feeling good, that is why I want to stay for some more time." I questioned her " Why are you feeling happy? Because you missed your school right?" she answered, "One of the reasons is that school got missed and another is that I felt good talking to you".

Listening to her answer I felt so good, but missing school is not a good thing and also she has misunderstood her mom's concern and caring as strictness, that made me think a bit but I told her to listen to her parents. She told me "Every day you come to the bus stop like this we will sit and talk". I replied to her "no dear, from tomorrow I will go in my vehicle. I came to the bus stop today because my bike got punctured".

She already missed her school and spent enough time away from home, her parents being unaware that she had missed her school, So I said to her "Go home safely, don't go here and there, directly go home". hearing me she felt a little but she finally understood my point and said bye she jumped from the bus stop platform and went home running, adjusting her school bag on her shoulders. She had such an adorable, innocent heart.

I was exceptionally tense about everything that was going on, office, transport and all but after conversing with her I felt so great. after she went I felt like I would have allowed her to sit and talk some little more time. I began feeling bored so I started checking my phone, At last, another bus showed up and again everyone assembled to get up on this. This time I didn't attempt to get that bus since I would have rather not gotten hit by once again. I thought to let people who are holding up urgency will go on this and I can go on another coming later this.

I saw that angry lady trying hard to catch the second bus, pushing other ladies aside, thank god I didn't attempt this time, else I would have got a nice tight slap on another cheek as well, in the urge of getting on the bus she didn't notice about her saree and its end got stuck in the door of the vehicle, unaware of that she just got up into the bus and her yellow saree with big red roses tore a little bit.

She didn't even realize it soon, she noticed it after she got on the bus, after realizing she started shouting, are you, ladies, out of your mind? look my beautiful saree got damaged because of you people, can't you people behave gently? I saw this all mess sitting on the bench itself, it all happened because of her own mistake but she charged at all. Well nobody in that bus seemed to care about her shouting, all were busy finding a seat and getting settled in the rush bus, meanwhile, the conductor whistled and the bus started.

childhood is a brilliant time, being children we check out issues in a simple manner and live cheerfully even in the most exceedingly terrible circumstance. I missed my childhood after meeting that girl, Indeed, even I began thinking like her, anyway has gotten late to office, how it would be if I take leave and rest at home.

I got up from the bench and started walking towards my home but again gave a second thought that there is no point in going back to home, however, I have come so far from home, and waited till now and if I go back, the time that already I have spent will go waste. I slowed my walk, in the dilemma of taking leave or not. meanwhile, an auto drew close to me sounding horn, the auto driver asked me, need auto? I stood quiet since I was considering withdrawing leave or not. The auto driver again asked, Where do you need to go? In the disarray of withdrawing or not, I chose to go to the workplace since I had arrived at the bus station, what's the point in returning home, so I took an auto.

I got into the auto and asked the driver to take me to the Majestic bus station. I settled myself and kept my PC pack on the seat adjacent to me, and I saw an old book with a dark green hardcover on the auto seat. I asked the driver "whose book is this?" the driver answered "I don't know madam", with a doubt I said "maybe your last traveler has left it here" with a confident voice driver replied, "No madam, you are my first passenger of the day".

Then, it may be the last person who traveled yesterday. I questioned him "Do you recollect who was your last traveler yesterday? the driver replied "I do recall, the previous evening I dropped a woman close to Vijaynagar metro station," the driver said. Holding that book in my right hand and turning around I said this book seems very old as its corners are a little bent, maybe that lady by mistake has forgotten this book in auto, who knows it might be important for her, and she might be unaware that she has forgotten in your auto. with an ignorant attitude driver replied, "Leave it madam, why you are worrying about that book and if it was that important, now wouldn't have left in the auto".

I asked the driver to give the at contact number of that lady if has with him, with denial he spoke: "No madam I don't have. I rarely talk to passengers, I ask for a destination address, for directions if required, then to collect my auto fare, otherwise, I don't talk to customers much". I replied to him "ok but how do you will return this book now?" With a surprised tone, the driver spoke " returning that is not possible I will just keep that book for one more day in auto if no one comes asking that I will just throw it."

I felt bad about what he said, don't throw it, you don't know whether it is important to book or not, The you keep it with you and return it said the driver. listening to him I felt a little bad though I was thinking about that lady what if she was searching for this book and don't even remember that she forgot in auto, I just sat quiet, the driver suggested: "Check-in that book madam, there might be any information written in the book." How can I check someone's book without her consent I replied. "Then leave it, madam. Why are you worried about, said the driver, he showed no interest in finding out the owner of the book nor worried about the belongings of passengers. " said the driver.

He questioned me " You are not ready to open the book then how will you come to know anything about the book owner". I replied, " Yes you are right, I will check the first and the last page may some info is written, which might help me find the owner of the book". saying this I was just about to open the book driver said " Get down madam, We reached the majestic bus stop."

I kept the book in a bag and went to the platform searching for the bus to go to the workplace. The majestic bus stop is the main junction point in Bangalore, and buses from all areas come here so I got the bus soon, luckily I got a seat, I sat on the seat by the window, I love sitting window-side while traveling, took out my phone to watch the news but network inclusion was low so I began checking my photos, after some time I got bored of seeing pics, so thought to keep the phone in the bag and take little travel nap since it would nearly take me one hour to arrive at the destination.

Though getting sleep in Bangalore city transport is not possible but I got to sleep as I was a little tired of all that stuff that happened at the bus stop and waiting long for catching the bus. The sudden break made me wake up, a stray dog suddenly came in front of the bus, because of which driver had broken the speed of the vehicle and passengers who were standing in the bus were about to fall many held the pillars in the bus to prevent themselves from falling, I too held support handle stiffly.

Now that dog crossed the road vehicle started moving, yet the office was so far, and I wasn't getting sleep back meanwhile I remembered that I have put someone's book in my bag, I took it out It was Moss green shading hardcover with a brilliant blueprint on it, "A piece of my life" composed on it in strong Italic brilliant letters, by book cover I could figure that it was an extremely old book, the sides of the book were little twist, seems as though she used to write in that book every day.

I was in dilemma concerning whether to open that book or not. I had just a single decision left was to check that book and get the data of that woman so I could return it to the proprietor of the book. At last, I chose to open it and read just first and last because generally, individuals compose their names and subtleties at the start or the finish of the book.

I turned the front of the book, the primary page was blank, turned one more, observed a blossom sketch, and got feeling like is it that important book for her or not? what if this is just a sketchbook. Did I argue do much with that auto driver for no reason? Was that driver right? was it would have been good if left it there in the auto, he would do whatever he had to do with this book.

I turned the third page, the fourth page, just found sketches, I opened the last page again a rose sketch, I got to realize that it's simply a sketchbook, it's a hobby and perhaps not that significant, if not, then, at that point, she would essentially think of writing her name or something in this book, I just shut the book and while keeping the book inside the bag I saw one bookmark of red glossy silk material trim. I opened that book at the bookmark, "I LIVED MINUTES OF DEATH" was written in body capital letters, though that sentence was scary but interesting too, how can a person live the minutes in death, I found it interesting and felt like reading it.

Turned page and the first title was written as " Marathon". firstly I found the title itself the most interesting and on that the first title is a marathon, I build curiosity within me to read the book so I started reading, I got to know that her name is " Tara" with the first line of the next chapter and rest is what she wrote.

MARATHON

5th May 2016 - Tara

My phone alarm had been snoozing for quite some time, so I woke up early in the morning, struggling to open my eyes forcibly to get up from incomplete sleep, hitting the snoozing alarm on my phone, took off the blanket, got up from bed, and as I touched my feet on the floor, I felt frigid, so I suddenly took my legs up on the bed and blanket back on me and slightly took off the blanket from my face and saw at the wall clock with half-opened eyes, It was 4:15 a.m., and I opened both eyes wide in surprise because I was supposed to get up at 4 a.m. according to my schedule.

I quickly got out of bed, gently took my phone so that if I dropped something by accident, my husband would be wake up by the sound; usually, I drop things in my sleep; thankfully, I didn't touch anything else on the table except my phone; I charged it, walked into the hall, and slowly closed the bedroom door.

I work in a BPO, and my office is an unusually long distance from my home. I spend a large portion of my day traveling; I begin my day early and end it late at night, and I barely get 5 to 6 hours of sleep in 24 hours.

Monday is a tough day for many in this entire universe and assuming you have an inquiry in your brain, why do I get up at 4 am? Since I need to prepare food and go to the workplace, I got up in the wake of napping my alert like clockwork right from 3:30 am. It takes me around 30 minutes to get rid of bed so early, it turns out to be exceptionally difficult to get up in a chilly environment.

Here I paused reading; after four paragraphs, I felt like tara had written this either to give to someone to read or to publish as a book or article; whatever she wrote, I found it interesting, and a little bit matching to every working woman; even I get up early and do household chores before leaving for work, this was relatable; without her consent, I began to learn about her. After another ten minutes, I resumed my reading.

Tara - If I'm riding my bike to work, I leave by 7 a.m.; if I'm taking the BMTC bus, which is Bangalore's local public transportation, I leave by 6 a.m.

Bangalore is a job hub; many people move to Bangalore for work, and they all leave their homes early in the morning to commute to their workplaces, and this metropolitan city is congested during peak hours in the morning and evening.

People in Bangalore typically use public transportation because it is less expensive than private vehicles, but it is also more time-consuming. Traveling by own vehicle saves half the time, and time is more expensive than money, so I began riding my bike to work instead of taking the bus.

Because I was traveling neighbors by work station my bike, I had three hours in the morning to complete household tasks such as cooking, cleaning, and ironing. I took a shower and then went into the kitchen.

First, I drank a glass of warm water. It makes me feel better in the cold, it's already been 30 minutes since I woke up, but I had so much work to do before going to the office, geared up, and started kitchen work.

For lunch every day, I make wheat flour chapatis. Assume I'm preparing lunch at 4:30 a.m.; mine is still normal; however, my neighbor's workstation the aunty washes clothes at 4 a.m. because she works in a garment factory; she leaves at 6 a.m. and returns at 9 p.m.

While everyone else is sleeping, only I and that aunty get up and start working; we don't talk that early, but hearing the sound of washing clothes gives me the courage to stand alone in the kitchen and work without fear.

When Aunty doesn't get up and I don't hear the sound of washing clothes, it's difficult for me because I'll be the only one awake at that time. Even looking out the window makes me nervous. The wind howling seemed terrifying to me at such times, but she was awake that day.

First, I made a wheat flour dough and set it aside for a few minutes while I chopped onions, tomatoes, and eggplant, cooked eggplant curry, it's a quick recipe for a curry with chapati if you're in a hurry, eggplants cook in less than 10 minutes.

After the curry, I put the rice in the cooker to cook and washed the utensils from the previous night's dinner. When I finished cleaning the dishes, the cooker whistled, so I turned it off and started making chapatis and veg fried rice. I packed lunch, set the boxes aside, and cooked breakfast. I make breakfast after lunch so that it is still warm by the time my husband eats it.

I kept my box in my bag and his on the dining table, I closed the lid on his breakfast and looked at the clock. It's already 6:30 a.m., and I have to leave the house by 7. I dressed quickly and dashed to the kitchen to make tea for my husband. I make it late so that it stays hot until he wakes up. I placed his tea and hot water mug on the table and dashed back to the bathroom, where I turned on the hot water for his bath.

My husband wakes up late; his office is only 6 to 7 km far, so he gets up around 7 to 7:30 a.m.; everything will be ready for him; all he has to do is take a bath, eat, and leave for work.

I took the bike and home keys, locked the door, we both kept one key with each other because our timings are different, none of us will be an in-home to open the door, He will open the door from inside while going to the office, we rarely get time to talk or spend time together, we don't even say good-bye while leaving for work.

It was already 6:58 a.m., so I flung to the bike, inserted the bike key, and was about to start the bike. On the way to the office, I came to the realization I had forgotten to bring the garbage bag to put in the dumping box.

I have to carry a garbage bag with me because I am not at home all day and a person who collects garbage from home comes around 8 a.m., so I have to carry it with me and dump it in a dumping box every day. I ran back home, opened the lock, took a garbage bag, and locked the door again before returning to the bike.

My mornings are nothing short of a marathon. I keep running until I get to the office, then I calm down once I get to my workstation, but then I have to deal with pressure from the team leader and others to keep up with my work. I sometimes have the impression that I am a machine.

My bike did not start with the starter button, the battery died due to the cold, I set the bike on a double strand, the bike is too heavy to lift on the second stand, and my energy was already depleted from household work since I worked from the time I woke up, but by striving, I eventually managed to put it on the main stand and the bike started after kicking 7 times.

I left home and stopped after one and a half km to dump the garbage. as I was standing back to my bike, a bike came and slightly hit my standing bike, two boys on that bike, maybe 14 years old. I don't understand why parents let children take bikes on roads, they are so young for getting on a bike on roads, a lady standing beside me yelled at those boys saying "Where are your parents? Who let you ride a bike like this outside, you kids are all still in school and you want bikes? "Those kids were scared and ran away from there quickly, but the lady did not stop yelling; I told her that perhaps their parents were unaware that their children were riding their bikes; I left from there because I was running late.

Morning and evening traffic will be heavier in Bangalore because it is a job hub, and all offices open at 9 a.m., so people will be rushing to get to work. Bangalore has a lot of traffic.

After 6 km, I noticed a traffic jam on the road. What happened? I asked a person making a U-turn in that traffic. He stated that one of the public transportation buses had stopped in the road due to an engine problem, which had caused the majestic road to be jammed for 30 minutes, vehicles were moving very slowly, I felt walking would be faster than driving, but I didn't have any other choice but to wait for traffic to clear, after the hard work of traffic police in convincing all vehicles to patiently make the way clear, traffic began to move. huh! I took a deep breath and slowly passed through the traffic. Riding a two-wheeler is easier than driving a car in Bangalore because two-wheelers can easily make way because they are smaller in size than four-wheelers.

OFFICE

I arrived at the office late, parking was full, and there was no space for even a single bike. I asked the watchman to clear some space for parking, and he said, "Sorry ma'am, I just sent two more ladies back to park their vehicles beside the road just now, there is no space left."

There was some space on campus, but there was a risk of parking because no watchman would be looking after vehicles parked there, but I had no choice and had to get to work. I was about to park the bike when I noticed someone exiting the lift. He took his bike and exited; I turned around and parked my bike in a vacant spot before going to the lift; however, the lift was full, so I ran to the stairs; finally, I entered my floor.

The locker room was full of gossiping girls, and one of my colleagues, Sneha, was there. She waved hello and asked why I was so late, to which I replied, "You know Bangalore traffic, right?" I kept my belongings in the locker and asked my colleague, "Come on, let's go," to which she replied, "Wait, I'll just apply lipstick and come." I told her she could come later. I'll go ahead and log in first. It was already too late, and I fled.

told her to come back later I'll go ahead and log in first. It was already too late, and I fled.

As I walked in, I noticed my team leader standing next to my workstation, asking about me to the person sitting next to me. I approached her and said in hushed tones, "I am here, good morning, ma'am."

I'm guessing my team leader had a very good morning because she smiled and said, "It's okay, I know you're a sincere employee, try coming soon tomorrow." I thanked her and got to work. My login time is 9 a.m., but I arrived at 9:45 a.m.

I started work, didn't have breakfast or tea, and the weather was cold, so I got a headache and a hungry stomach that wasn't letting me work properly, but I dragged myself until the first break that I took at 11 a.m., I get one hour of break time and I can divide it however I want, usually 15 minutes in the morning, 30 minutes for lunch, and 15 minutes in the evening.

Author - Here I paused reading again due to disruption, at one stop more passengers boarded the bus, and the bus became too crowded and noisy, so I just kept that book inside the bag, took out my headphones, and began listening to music. After reading her book so far, I realized that her life is quite similar to mine, getting up early in the morning, cooking, traveling, working, and so on. I was reading someone else's book without her permission; my intention before starting to read that book was only to find her contact information, but after reading a little, I found it interesting and got carried away.

In my office, I told a friend about this book and everything, and she said, "Read it completely, you might get any contact information." "But I've already read so much that I didn't get it, and what if I don't get it?" I replied. "If you don't get an address or phone number, just read it and give it to some old newspaper collector," a friend advised.

When my phone's battery died in the evening, I went back to that book to see if I could find any more details. I just kept turning pages, and on the last four pages, I saw one email address. When I got home, the first thing I did was open my laptop and type an email that said, hello, I found one book today morning in an auto, I tried searching for an address or contact details in the book but I didn't find any details except this email id, If this book belongs to you, please contact on the number below.

The next day, I left the book at home. I rode my bike to the office. My day at work went well, and I was relieved to have a normal day. It wasn't like yesterday's adventure. I waited all day for that lady to call and ask for her book. I'm not sure if she read the email, but there was no call from an unknown number on my phone.

I took my laptop to watch a movie, and before I started it, I checked my inbox to see if there were any new emails; there were none, but while I was watching the movie, I received a notification of an email, which I opened; it was a reply to my previous email, which said, Hi, my name is Tara, and this is my book; I lost it the day before yesterday; thank you for informing me. We had a conversation via e-mail.

I apologized for reading her book without her permission, and she replied, "It's okay, don't be sorry, there's nothing secret in that book, I just wrote about the accident that I met." Wanting to know I inquired, "Accident?" Oh my goodness! When did it take place? "It's already been a year," Tara responded. "Are you writing it to publish a book?" I questioned. she responded "No, that scene keeps replaying in my head, and it's upsetting. While I was feeling down about the accident, a friend suggested that I write everything down in a book or on paper and destroy it somewhere".

"Why do you want to destroy it?" I asked. "Yes, my friend told me to burn it or throw it," she replied. I was surprised to hear that something we wanted to forget had been written down and destroyed, so I asked her again, "Are you sure you want to destroy it?" She replied, "Yeah, I'm sure." I asked her, "Rather than throwing it, I'd like to keep it with me, so could you please allow me to keep it?"

"Why do I want to keep it?" Tara inquired. I told her that I am a writer and that I would like to write a book about this event. "Anyway, that incident is no longer mine because I wrote it intending to destroy it, and I am delighted to hear that you will be writing a book," she replied.

It was clear to me whether I should continue reading or not, but I didn't have enough time, so I planned to take the bus again just to read that book because I would be sitting idle on the bus, and it would be great if I could use that time for reading.

The next morning, I took that book with me and bought some chocolates thinking that cute girl would see me again, went to the bus stop, everything was normal unlike the other day, the bus was already on the platform, but I didn't go in that bus because I arrived early so I could go next bus, but I was looking for that little girl rakshita, wasn't aware she had gone to school or hasn't come to bus stop yet.

I was sitting on a bench, looking at my phone, when that girl came to the bus stop. She was wearing a tracksuit this time and was overjoyed. She didn't seem to notice me. I approached her and said, "Hello, Rakshita." She was overjoyed to see me return, she said "Hello, Akka, are you here? I wasn't expecting you to show up "I told her I had come to meet her, and as she listened to me, she was overjoyed. I inquired of her "What happened to your uniform? Are you not going to school today?" "I'm having a sports day today, so I'm wearing a tracksuit," she said with a big smile on her face.

When I offered her chocolates, she refused, saying, "My mummy will scold me if I take chocolates." "Yes, your mummy is correct, one should not take anything from strangers, and she chastises you for your goodness," I replied. She sadly nodded her head down because she loves chocolates and wanted to take them but couldn't because her mom said she couldn't take anything from strangers, so I told her, "Keep these chocolates with you but don't eat them now, once you go back home, tell your mom about me, and eat chocolates only if she allows." Happily, she took the chocolate and stored it in her sports bag.

A bus pulled up. We both got on that bus, she got off after four stops, and I continued the journey, taking out that book and starting reading it from where I left off. Tara went on to write the following.

Tara-

I had two boxes with me, one for breakfast and one for lunch. I went to the cafeteria for breakfast, began eating, and noticed my friend waiting at the food counter to purchase food for her. She doesn't bring food because she stays in a hostel.

I invited her to join, and she said, "You go ahead, I'll bring food." I finished half of my breakfast, but she was still standing in line, checking her wristwatch because break time was flying by.

I approached her and invited her to join me for breakfast because there are so many people waiting in line and the server is serving slowly. If things continue like this, you will have food by lunchtime. She laughed and said, "Yes, you're correct, let's go."

When we arrived at the table, I offered her my other box to eat, but she refused, saying, "I know it's your lunch box, how can I have that, what will you have for lunch?" We are not in the jungle, I replied, we will get food, it's just that right now we are running out of time, we will have 30 minutes in lunch break we can buy food so don't worry, common have it now we are getting late listening to this she agreed and we had breakfast and went back to work.

The server went down at noon, so we took a short break from work. The team leader announced that everyone should go get lunch now so that they can work during their lunch break later.

Everyone started screaming no no no because whenever the server goes down, it's time for everyone to enjoy some gup shup. It was 12:30 p.m., and we usually take a lunch break after 1 p.m., so we sat idle with coworkers.

Everyone started screaming no no no because whenever the server goes down, it's time for everyone to enjoy some gup shup. It was 12:30 p.m., and we usually take a lunch break after 1 p.m., so we sat idle with coworkers. the server took a long time to restart, we had plenty of time for lunch. We ate lunch at 2 p.m., returned, and the server began serving at 2:45 p.m.

As I had logged in late that day, I had to log out late to make up for the time difference, and it was raining heavily that evening, so everyone was sitting there in the office itself waiting for the rain to stop, and everyone was enjoying. After finishing my work, I joined them all, and all were having a good time. I was worried I'd be late because I had a long drive ahead of me and couldn't join in on their fun. I went to look out the window to see when the rain would stop. I saw the beautiful rain view from the window from the 6th floor, the rain on empty roads was a beautiful view, and getting to see empty roads in Bangalore is a very rare possibility, even at night, many vehicles will be on roads.

I sat with my colleagues, waiting for an hour, and it seemed like it would rain all night. I decided to leave for home because it was getting late for me, my home was a long distance away from my work location, and traffic is heavier in Bangalore at this time of day because almost all office logout times are the same in the evening.

My colleagues were still chit-chatting in the office, enjoying the rain, but I left from there, saying goodbye to everyone; as I came out of my floor, I could hear a loud storm and lightning.

I came out of the office, saw the lift was open, someone had just left it open and gone, I quickly stepped in a hurry so it didn't close its door and I had to open it again, pressed the G floor button, and the door was slowly closing, meanwhile heard a voice from afar, a girl screaming wait for me, wait for me waving one hand up in the air, as I heard and saw her running towards the lift, I suddenly put my left leg in between the closing door but I got scared for a second thinking about what might happen, so I quickly removed my leg from there and held my lunch box bag in the middle of the door with my right hand in the air, and the door slowly opened; now that the door was open, I kept my leg and told her to come quickly.

That girl was wearing blue jeans and a white top, running towards the lift with her backpack lifted; as she approached, her footsteps were audible; she came in and said thank you for stopping for me in a heavy voice; I said first calm down and settle yourself; it's just that I was in the lift; anyone in my position would do the same; which floor do you want to go? She waved her index finger and said first floor, then smiled and asked what department you worked in. I was telling her about my department, and when we got to the first floor, she said thank you again, and she left. She appeared to be in a rush.

Lift door closed and it started moving and there was a sudden glitch of light in the lift, I got scared like hell and my heart was in my mouth, I was shocked, so many thoughts were roaming in my mind what do I do if lift got stuck, more freaking was that I was alone in the lift, bad thoughts started floating in my mind meanwhile lift stuck, literally my eyes were filled with tears, I held breath remembered God! Saying ya God save me, I took out my phone from my bag to call office personnel and inform them that I was caught in a lift. As I took my phone out, the lift began, and I realized that my phone did not even have a network, so I would have been trapped in the lift until someone else arrived.

As I approached parking, I noticed a few people waiting for the rain to stop; trust me, seeing people there gave me some strength; that lift incident had made me freak out badly; even though I didn't know anyone standing there, I felt a little relaxed because after that lift thing happened, I felt like I was almost in a different world; I went to my bike and then realized I hadn't bought my raincoat, so I decided to wait a few more minutes in parking.

It was 7:30 p.m. when I checked my phone. It was getting late for me, and the rain didn't seem to be stopping, so I decided to go home in the rain. I locked the bag and phone in the bike trunk below the seat and tried to start the bike with the starter, but it didn't work. The following morning, I encountered the same problem, so I started the bike manually with a kick, but it did not start.

RAINY ROADS

I came out of the parking lot and saw that the entire road was empty, not even a single bicycle on the road, only a Bangalorean who travels daily can understand the happiness of riding a bike on empty roads in Bangalore, the rain was slowly reducing and as the rain was reducing one by one vehicle started coming on the road, but as people came out on the road seeing that the rain was lowering down, the rain started heavily again, now that people have already come on the road.

Bangalore The metro is up flyovers, so for people riding two-wheelers, the metro tracks are more like a roof, with many vehicles parked beneath it. Although I was completely wet, I stood there for a few minutes because the rain was very rough, it seemed like someone up there was very angry and taking revenge on humans by showing hatred in heavy rain, such a heavy rain it was that almost the entire road became invisible from everywhere I could see only rain and feel cold, and even a fully covered helmet was not enough to protect me from the rain, water splash passing my helmet on my cheeks felt like a tight slap on the face, after a while, it wasn't just rain, but the wind as well, and some of the umbrellas flew away with the force of the wind.

After a few minutes, the rain subsided slightly, and I proceeded to leave. After 5 kilometers, I received a red light signal; due to the rain, it took too long to cross that signal; there was too much traffic that day; by the time I arrived near the zebra crossing to pass the signal, it had already been thrice the red light and green light queue; finally, I arrived near the zebra crossing, pedestrians were crossing the road, a car arrived beside me, and the car side mirror was about to touch my bike handle.

When I looked at the red light's clock, it showed 5 seconds until the green light, so I prepared to leave. As I was about to speed up my bicycle, the car driver sped up and collided with his vehicle's side mirror. It hit me forcefully, and I was about to fall, but I figured out how to hold the bicycle with the help of my body weight and left from there.

Around 500 meters later, there was heavy traffic due to rainwater on the road in the bridge's underpass, and I saw the same car, so I went beside the driver's mirror and knocked on the mirror, as the window slid down and the man in the driver seat looked at me interrogatively before he could say anything. What if I fell because you hit my bike handle with your car's side mirror? He apologized, saying, "I didn't realize, I didn't do it on purpose, I'm sorry."

Hearing him, I realized he was aware that he had hit my bike handle, but he didn't even apologize for doing so there and then, and he wasn't sorry until I went to him. What if I trip and fall? He apologized once more, madam. I decided it was pointless to argue when he was apologizing, so I dropped the subject and moved on.

The rain got worse with time, thunderstorms and lightning scared me, and the power went out all over the city due to heavy rainfall, it seemed like a bad time, only vehicle lights were on all around, but within 15 minutes power was restored and all street lights were turned on.

ACCIDENT

I was stuck in another signal after another 12 kilometers. I was in the very last row of traffic, far away from the zebra crossing. Two girls were riding on a bike that came up beside me. Both girls were completely soaked, just like me, and the girl behind me was shivering from the cold, holding both hands close to her chest with folded arms.

The girl on her bike approached me and asked for directions to the Majestic bus stop. I said, "Well, it's about 10 kilometers from here, I'm going on the same way, you can follow me," she replied with a tired sound, and another person I asked for directions in the last signal said the same thing to follow him. We did follow him for a while, but his bike and he don't know how and where disappeared in traffic.

I'm new to Bangalore and have no idea where to go. I considered using Google Maps, but due to the rain, I am unable to take my phone out of the bike trunk. Her voice was shivering, and she was speaking loudly so that I could hear her, the rain sound was louder.

I noticed her hands gripping the handle of the bike; her hands, like her voice, were shivering; it appears that they have been in the rain for a long time. I realized I'd be like her cold arrested until I got home, so I silently prayed to God for mercy and to help me get home safely.

I said to her, "Look, sister, I understand your situation right now in the rain." There are so many turns and signals to cross before you reach majestic; obviously, I can't guide them all at once, and even if I did, it wouldn't stick with you for long.

If you feel like following a single-vehicle is difficult because of traffic, you can just keep on asking different people at turns and reach the destination, with a sad face she said hmm I don't have any other choice but I request you to go slow so that I can follow you.

I gave her a thumbs up and said, "OK, I'll be slow, and I'll keep looking at your bike from my mirror." As I finished my conversation, I noticed that the light had turned green, and all vehicles began moving; I told the girl to pass the signal and wait for me because I had a car in front of me that was moving slowly; she replied, "I'll wait for you after the signal there," and she went fast. As I mentioned, I was the last vehicle and there were no vehicles behind me, so I slowly started heading towards the end of the signal and signal green light time was one minute left and it was enough for the current vehicle in the signal to cross the signal within green light, meanwhile, I noticed a car coming behind honking, and in the right mirror, I saw two lights it was far and signal time was about to expire. so the car coming was supposed to wait in red light to pass the signal.

While passing the green light and turning right, the car behind me sped up and hit my right handle while crossing at the same green light, causing me to fall with my bike.

The car's back left wheel was about to collide with my helmet. As I fell, I was numb, my eyes were closed, I could hear vehicles honking too loudly, along with people screaming, accident, a car hit the bike, the lady is dead, oh my god it's on the spot death, oh no she is bleeding, all these sounds in my ear but in my mind, something else was happening, no one came near me, all were standing so far away from me, and vehicles were still passing by my side without looking that human is laying.

My body stopped moving, my eyes closed, and images of people from my life came one after the other like a slideshow, including my mother, father, husband, sisters, brother, childhood playing images, and so on.

It was so fast that all images were disappearing and fleeing from my eyes, leaving me alone, not only family images, but I also saw many other random images that I don't remember or hadn't seen before, I don't know what that all was and I could hear so many random sounds that were very unpleasant and scary, while this was all happening in my mind the people sound and screaming and everything was just absent.

I felt like I was going somewhere, there was no pain in my body, I was very light at the weight, and then everything vanished, leaving only full light, nothing else visible, and I was just blank. After all, based on what was happening to me, I convinced myself that "I AM DEAD."

At the time, I was attempting to recall my mother and father but was unable to do so. I tried to cry but nothing happened to me; I tried to scream but received no response from my senses. What I felt, what I experienced, trust me, I can't put it into words, I can't express that feeling of losing everything and yet being unable to feel it the way we humans do, only white light flashing on and off, I tried calling Allah for help, I tried screaming Allah, but all I could see was light, nothing else. Now I stopped trying everything because I was convinced in my mind that I was no longer alive. After a while, I felt a sudden hard-hitting jerk on me and woke up with a scream, feeling as if I could breathe again.

When I opened my eyes, everything was blurry. Two men came running towards me, but I couldn't see them. As they got closer, I realized they were traffic cops, and one of them was a young boy who had just finished school. The officer waved his right hand in front of my face and asked, "Are you all right?" I couldn't respond to him, so I just blinked my eyes, and I saw that my leg was stuck beneath my bike. The police took his speaker and announced that they would take their vehicles from the other side of the road and clear the chaos of people standing around to see what was going on.

People were standing there as if they were watching some kind of entertainment show as if they had paid to watch and enjoy a human lying down on the road who had died in an accident.

Are you in a condition to get up, the cops asked? Should I call an ambulance now that I can see him? He was dressed in the uniform, with a speaker in his hand and a head cap on. I showed him thumbs and said ok, I am ok, I am fine, listening to this traffic police, he took his speaker and started screaming clear the traffic, and guided them to take right and left accordingly, two more people came and took off my bike aside, in the meantime, that boy came and helped me get up, he made me sit on the footpath, I thanked him for helping me, and he left from there and saw my gown was torn on the right leg side and my slipper.

This is the harsh reality of metropolitan cities: people pass by a dying person but no one comes forward to help, and the car driver flees at full speed without even looking at what he has done, so cruel that people watch it like drama instead of coming forward for help. Usually, many people take images and post on social media that an accident occurred, but will not call an ambulance for an emergency, they record video and post on status and stories but will not give a helping hand.

I was in pain when I noticed that my slippers were filled with blood as I kept them aside and the bloodstains on them washed off with rain, and my leg was still bleeding, so I sat back and thought to call my husband, so I opened bike trunk and took the phone to call, but I remembered that my husband also logs out at the same time, and he might be on his way home and will not be able to take my call, so I thought to call anyone else but in Bangalore, we are the only two people staying in the home, me and my husband, therefore I kept back my phone in the bag and closed the bike trunk.

I decided to go home, as I sat on the bike holding the handle, I noticed that the bike handle was slightly moved on one side, I tried to align it center and it got a little better, this time with God's grace bike started with starter, suppose if it failed to ignite with a starter I wasn't in condition to start it with a kick, my right leg was injured, I left from there, my leg pained badly when I took it up on bike footrest, I cried in pain and prayed God to make me reach home soon.

Almost majestic When I saw the girls who had asked me for directions, they came closer to me and said, "You disappeared too." I apologised for not being able to show you the way to your destination. "We waited for you, but you didn't come, and traffic police sent us from there, saying don't stand here, a girl was hit by a car here, go safely." said the girl "Yes, I was there" I replied, she asked "Did you see that girl who died on the spot of the accident?" who told you that girl met with an accident has died? I questioned that bike girl for which she replied " I heard people talking there so I asked you, as you told you were there" Angrily I replied, "No it's not true, I am alive and standing right in front of you."

She inquired about it "What exactly? Was it you who has met the accident?" Yes, I said. listening to me she replied " Oh my Jesus! Now, are you?" I replied " I am fine" Take care, and I apologize for bothering you in this situation, but could you please show us the way to majestic? asked that bike girl. I replied "you have already reached majestic, just take right and it's majestic." to which she replied "Shit! Thank you, finally, we reached. You to reach home safely, bye." They took right and I continued my way home.

While all of this was going on, time flew by and it was too late; I'm not sure what time it was, but all of the shops on the road were closing one by one, and I couldn't find a single medical shop on the road until I got close to my house and the rain began to subside. Finally, I found one medical shop about 2 kilometers away and stopped there.

I took out my wallet and went to the medical shop. I purchased gauze, cotton, ointment, and some pain killer medicine, I knew some medicine and had some knowledge of first aid, shopkeeper delayed to generating the bill, he told me that he is having some issue with his computer, I told him that I am injured, take money without generating bill, later do the necessary, but he denied to do so, he took around 20 minutes for him to set all things and generate the bill, finally, I paid the bill and came to bike.

What is going on with me? Why should I? All of this has happened to me since the morning, and it has made me feel very bad and low. Now my energy is depleted, and I want to cry in pain but can't because I'm in a public place.

"Sir, my bike is not starting with a starter, and my leg is injured, so I am unable to start with a kick, can you please help me?" I returned to the shopkeeper. He replied, "Hmm, I will assist, but the customer is waiting for the bill, and as you know, the computer is having some issues, so your bill was generated so late." It sounded like he wasn't willing to help, so I told him, "It's okay, no problem, I'll manage." Meanwhile, the customer standing nearby heard me and said, "Sister, wait, I'll help you," and he started the bike with a kick. I thanked him for his assistance, and he replied, "It's okay, sister."

BACK TO PAVILION

I finally made it home. I parked my bike and noticed that the front door was open; my husband had returned home before me; I called out to him; he didn't hear me, I guess; he didn't respond to me; I went inside; he wasn't in the hall; he was in the room and was wearing headphones, watching something on the laptop; as I entered, he saw me and removed his headphones.

He yelled angrily, "I called you multiple times on your phone since I got home, but there has been no response from you; one should have at least the common sense to answer calls."

He was worried about me not arriving home on time, and it was raining, so I told him I met an accident on the way home.

My husband became tense and inquired, "How did it happen?" "All of a sudden, a car came up behind me and hit the handle of my bike," I explained. He inquired "What happened? How?" I responded "I'm not sure how it happened; it just happened. (in a tense voice)" My husband told me to calm down and asked, "Did you take down the license plate number?"

I responded "No, I couldn't," she said, to which her husband replied, "OK, leave it, how are you feeling now?" Should we go to the hospital?" I replied that I was fine and that there was no need for me to go to the hospital. I brought some medicine and first aid supplies with me when I came.

My husband made the dressing and asked me to sleep; he also gave me a tablet that I requested, a pain reliever, but I was hungry as well, so my husband told me that he would bring something to eat from the kitchen; I stopped him, saying that whatever I cooked in the morning, I packed for lunch and that I would cook fresh for dinner after I returned from work.

"I will order food online, you take tablets only after eating, otherwise you will feel stomach discomfort," the husband said. "Wait, look at the time now, all food restaurants will be closed, let it be I will cook after some time," I responded

My husband expressed regret and said "How will you cook now that you're injured? I also don't know how to cook " I replied, "It's okay, no problem, I'll manage, I'll take some rest, and then I'll go cook the food.", he asked me if there is Maggi in-home cause he knew cooking Maggi, but unfortunately, Maggi was not available in the home, so I told him not to worry give me few minutes, he asked me to take some rest.

I rested for 25 minutes before going to the kitchen to prepare only rice and daal. We both ate dinner, and because my husband was worried about me, he took plates to the kitchen, made me feel better, and asked me to sleep.

Despite having had a long and exhausting day, I finally made it home. I was missing my mother terribly. Because it was late, I considered calling her. I didn't call because I was afraid she'd be worried if I called late at night.

I inquired about my husband's day. He said it was normal as usual, office work, boring routine, same as usual, even he gets tired by the end of the day so I asked him to sleep, even though he was sleepy and trying to console me. My entire day had been a roller coaster, and that incident was flashing through my mind as I tried to sleep. Seeing me struggle, my husband asked, "What is that stopping you from sleeping?" tears in my eyes, and I replied, "People standing there were simply standing there looking at me, no one came near to help me, and the fact that people were busy taking pics on the phone rather than using their phones to call an emergency."

"That's harsh, but it's the reality of the situation; no one comes forward for help, but you're fine now, so don't think too much; try getting some sleep, you're tired," my husband said. What would have happened if I had truly died, and who would have informed you? My husband responded, "Now don't think about that, and stop thinking in a negative way, nothing has happened, and with God's grace you are fine, so just sleep."

I consider myself fortunate to have him by my side at all times. After a few minutes of conversation, he fell asleep, but I couldn't sleep. My mind was jumbled by everything that had happened to me, and everything was swirling around in my head.

Whatever happened, it was fated to happen; I had no control over it. I consoled myself and finally fell asleep after hours of trying.

My body was in excruciating pain the next morning, and I could barely walk, so I took leave, and my husband also took leave to care for me. We spent the day together, and I gradually began to feel better.

CONCLUSION

Tara, a working woman, runs a full day to meet her professional and personal obligations; she is brave enough to overcome the incident that occurred to her; the entire day was not good for her, but she never gave up hope, and she ended her day on a positive note as a responsible wife.

It is a harsh reality that people watch accidents for entertainment, and many will record the incident on their phones, but no one will come forward for assistance. The worst thing that people do is post images of other people's images in that condition.

The card driver who hit her didn't show a decent courtesy of checking on what he has done, a mistake happened by humans and that is quite natural but facing the mistake what has happened is real humanity.

After reading Tara's book, I felt that this story needed to be told so that people could understand how painful it is when people leave a body unattended on the road and how it feels when you don't have anyone to console you. Tara is a brave lady who stayed strong after all of this, her mental trauma from the accident caused her to suffer a lot, she fought it alone, and I hope she overcomes it.

Life is hectic, but it is meaningless without your loved ones; it takes a little bit of care and love to be showered on each other to make life happen.

We don't know what will happen to us in the next second, so live every moment of your life to the fullest, try to be happy, and keep your surroundings happy.

When someone has an accident, instead of immediately posting it on social media, call an ambulance and, if necessary, the police.

Obey all traffic rules.

www.ingramcontent.com/pod-product-compliance
Lightning Source LLC
LaVergne TN
LVHW050424160726